Anatomy of a HURRICANE

by Terri Dougherty

Velocity is published by Capstone Press,
151 Good Counsel Drive, P.O. Box 669, Mankato, Minnesota 56002.
www.capstonepub.com

Library of Congress Cataloging-in-Publication Data

Dougherty, Terri.
Anatomy of a hurricane / by Terri Dougherty.
p. cm. — (Velocity. disasters)
Includes bibliographical references and index.
Summary: "Describes how hurricanes form, how scientists study them, and how
people can protect against their destruction"—Provided by publisher.
ISBN 978-1-4296-4795-3 (library binding)
1. Hurricanes—Juvenile literature. I. Title. II. Series.
QC944.2.D72 2011
551.55'2—dc22   2010014663

Editorial Credits
Jennifer Fretland VanVoorst, editor; Heidi Thompson, designer; Svetlana Zhurkin,
     media researcher; Eric Manske, production specialist

Photo Credits
Alamy/Jeff Greenberg, 11 (bottom); AP Photo/Alex Brandon, 36–37; AP Photo/Marcio Jose
Sanchez, 35 (top); Capstone Press, 8–9, 13 (middle), 20–21, 23 (middle), 32–33 (map);
Dreamstime/Federico Montemurro, 31; Getty Images/AFP/Matthew Hinton, 44–45; Getty
Images/AFP/Robert Sullivan, 41; Getty Images/Dave Einsel, 28; Getty Images/Joe Raedle, 26;
Getty Images/Scott Olson, 17; Getty Images/Stone/Charles Doswell III, 16; Getty Images/Taxi/
Terry Qing, cover (bottom); iStockphoto/Brad Ellis, 5 (top); iStockphoto/Donald Gruener,
4–5; iStockphoto/Jonas Marcos San, 43 (left); iStockphoto/Joseph Nickischer, 32 (bottom);
iStockphoto/Murat Giray Kaya, 43 (bottom); Library of Congress, 14 (top); NASA, 11 (middle),
12–13; Newscom, 29; NOAA, 14–15, 19, 24–25, 27, 30, 33 (top), 34, 35 (bottom); NOAA/
Dr. Terry McTigue, NOAA, NOS, ORR, 38–39; NOAA/Lieut. Commander Mark Moran,
NOAA Corps, NMAO/AOC, 5 (bottom), 10–11, 39 (top); NOAA/Tim Loomis/NESDIS/
Environmental Visualization Program, cover (top), 22–23; Photodisc, 6–7; Shutterstock/Kim
Reinick, 43 (top right); Shutterstock/Lisa F. Young, 42 (bottom); Shutterstock/Nikonov (metal
background), throughout; Shutterstock/Oculo (mosaic design element), cover and throughout;
Shutterstock/Scott Rothstein, 42 (middle); Shutterstock/Sebastian Kaulitzki (scratched metal
background), back cover and throughout; Shutterstock/Stacie Stauff Smith Photography, 40;
Shutterstock/Stanislav E. Petrov (cement background), throughout

TABLE OF CONTENTS

DAY OF DESTRUCTION

Roaring winds pushed sheets of rain. Trees twisted and toppled. Huge waves gushed onto land, sweeping away cars and homes.

People feared for their lives as they huddled in attics and on rooftops. Some were forced to swim for higher ground. They pushed away **debris** that floated by with the current.

When Hurricane Katrina hit the Gulf Coast on the morning of August 29, 2005, it brought destruction and death. Hurricanes are some of the most powerful natural disasters on Earth. The ruin Katrina caused is proof of the power of these destructive storms.

The word "hurricane" comes from Hunraken, the name for the Mayan storm god.

AUGUST 23, 2005: Katrina develops in the southeastern Bahamas.

AUGUST 25, 2005: Katrina hits southern Florida. Nine people are killed, and 1.2 million people lose power.

AUGUST 28, 2005: Katrina heads toward the Gulf Coast. The storm's winds reach 175 miles (282 kilometers) per hour.

AUGUST 29, 2005: Katrina hits a wide area of the Gulf Coast, where it loses strength. Levees in New Orleans, Louisiana, give way, flooding the city. The storm is blamed for more than 1,500 deaths and $81 billion in damage.

LEVEES

debris   remains of something that has been destroyed

levee   a bank built up to prevent flooding

5

Chapter 1

A LOOK INSIDE

EQUATOR

Recipe for a Hurricane

A hurricane needs the right conditions to develop. For a hurricane to form, it takes:

Distance from the equator: For a hurricane to grow, the storm must be at least 300 miles (483 km) from the equator. Here, Earth's movement causes the storm to begin spinning. If the storm is too close to the equator, Earth's rotation won't affect it, and a hurricane won't develop.

> 300 MILES
(> 483 KM)

FACT

In the Northern Hemisphere, Earth's rotation causes hurricanes to spin in a counterclockwise direction. In the Southern Hemisphere, however, the winds are pulled in the opposite direction. This means the hurricane turns clockwise.

Cool atmosphere: The warm water vapor cools as it moves upward. It **condenses** and turns into tiny water droplets. The droplets form clouds that develop into thunderstorms.

Proper wind movement: Light, spiraling winds help the storm become a hurricane. If the wind blows too hard, the storm will break up.

Warm ocean water: Hurricanes form when the ocean is at least 80 degrees Fahrenheit (27 degrees Celsius). At this temperature, the **atmosphere** above the water becomes unstable, and thunderstorms are created.

Humid air: Hurricanes need enough moisture to keep the thunderstorms going. Dry air makes it difficult for a hurricane to form.

> 80°F
(> 27°C)

condense—to turn from a gas into a liquid
atmosphere—the mass of air surrounding Earth

Tropical Fury

The storm that becomes a hurricane begins in the **tropics** as a group of thunderstorms. The thunderstorms begin to gather and spin around a center of low pressure. Warm, moist air rises. As it condenses, it feeds the storm clouds. Air rushes toward the low pressure area, and the storm gains strength. The hurricane grows as long as it has the right wind pattern and warm, moist air as fuel.

When hurricanes form in the western Pacific Ocean, they are known as **TYPHOONS.**

HURRICANES

TROPICAL CYCLONES are hurricanes that form in the Indian Ocean, Bay of Bengal, and Australia.

STAGES OF DEVELOPMENT

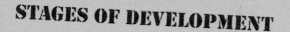

Before a storm reaches hurricane strength, it goes through several stages:

1. Tropical disturbance: a weather system that begins in the tropics or subtropics. The system of clouds and rain is active for 24 hours or more. It slightly turns around an area of low pressure.
2. Tropical depression: a storm with a long-lasting surface wind of less than 39 miles (63 km) per hour. The tropical **cyclone** is spinning around an area of low pressure.
3. Tropical storm: a tropical cyclone with a top wind speed that ranges from 39 to 73 miles (63 to 117 km) per hour
4. Hurricane: a tropical cyclone with winds of at least 74 miles (119 km) per hour.

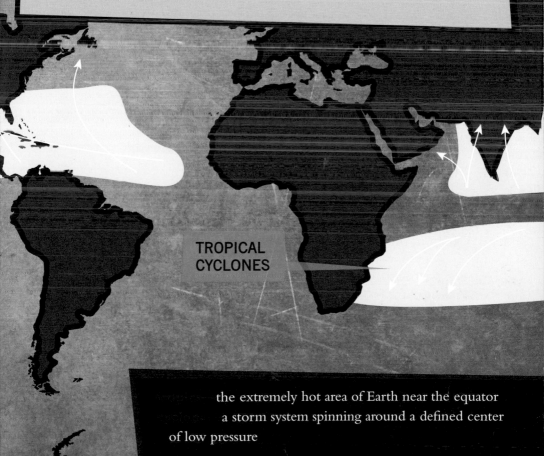

TROPICAL
CYCLONES

the extremely hot area of Earth near the equator
a storm system spinning around a defined center
of low pressure

Naming the Storm

Once a tropical weather system reaches wind speeds of 39 miles (63 km) per hour, it is given a name. Hurricanes were first named after Catholic saints or the location they made landfall. But during World War II (1939–1945), U.S. military forecasters started using women's names for storms. This method was picked up by the National Hurricane Center in 1953. In 1978, men's names were added to the list.

FACT! There are no names for the letters Q, U, X, Y, and Z. Sometimes there are more than 21 storms in one year. Then the letters of the Greek alphabet are used as storm names.

The World Meteorological Organization (WMO) puts together the storm name list. Each year, storms are named in alphabetical order, starting with the letter A. The names trade off between male and female names. In years that end with an even number, the storm name list starts with a man's name. In years that end with an odd number, the first storm is named after a woman.

The names of extremely destructive hurricanes are retired. This is done out of respect for people who were hurt or killed by the storm. The WMO decides when a name is retired.

Here are the 10 most recently retired names, and the year the storm hit:

2005
KATRINA
RITA
STAN
WILMA

2007
DEAN
FELIX
NOEL

2008
GUSTAV
IKE
PALOMA

Eye of the Storm

With winds that can top 150 miles (241 km) per hour, a hurricane is not exactly peaceful and quiet. However, the storm's center is calm.

The middle of the hurricane is known as the eye. When the eye of a storm passes over an area, the rain stops. The wind becomes light and calm. Often, the storm clouds are gone and blue sky or stars can be seen.

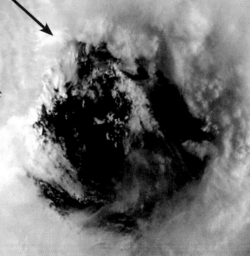

EYE OF THE HURRICANE

But the calm does not last. After the eye passes over the area, the other side of the storm hits. The eyewall is the band of clouds that surrounds the eye. It is the most powerful part of the storm.

Sometimes a storm has two eyewalls. A band of light rain separates the inner and outer rings of heavy rainfall. Inside the inner eyewall is the calm eye. Eventually the inner eyewall becomes weak and falls apart. It is replaced by the outer eyewall.

- **Eye**: This calm area is around 20 to 40 miles (32 to 64 km) across. The air in the center of the eye slowly sinks. The air here is warmer than in the rest of the storm, and the air pressure is lower. Air pressure is the force of air's weight pressing down on Earth's surface.

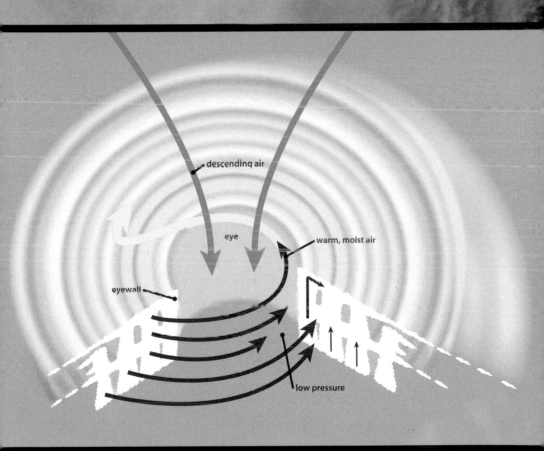

descending air

eye

warm, moist air

eyewall

low pressure

- **Eyewall**: The fiercest part of the storm rages here. The wall cloud around the eyewall can be 10 miles (16 km) high. The air rapidly moves up and down as the wind shifts fiercely. Most of the time, the warm moist air in the eyewall is moving upward.

Storm Surge

A hurricane unleashed its power on Galveston Island, Texas, the night of September 8, 1900. The storm toppled trees, crushed homes, and swept people into the ocean.

hurricane damage in Galveston, Texas, 1900

The storm surge was responsible for much of the damage and death in Galveston that night. A storm surge is a dome of water pushed by a hurricane. It is usually 50 to 100 miles (80 to 161 km) wide. It can be taller than a two-story house.

16 FEET
(5 M)

In 1899, Tropical Cyclone Mahina set a storm surge record. It hit Australia's coast with a dome of water more than 40 feet (12 m) high. The storm surge was so large that fish and dolphins were later found on top of cliffs.

A storm surge is the most dangerous part of a hurricane. Nine out of 10 hurricane victims die in the storm surge. A **high tide** made the Galveston storm surge especially destructive. As many as 12,000 people died in the Galveston hurricane.

high sea level caused by the pull of the sun and the moon on Earth

Hurricane Eloise hit Florida's panhandle in 1975.

Moving Inland

A hurricane hits land with great force. But it begins to lose steam after it hits the shore. It can no longer get energy from the warm ocean water.

On land, a hurricane's wind speeds may decrease. It may weaken to a tropical storm. However, it is still dangerous. Its winds may reach far inland. And almost all hurricanes that hit land in the United States bring at least one tornado. In 2004 Hurricane Ivan was responsible for 127 tornadoes along the Atlantic and Gulf coasts.

FACT

Hurricanes can create tornadoes thousands of miles away. A hurricane that makes landfall along the Atlantic Coast can spawn tornadoes in the Midwest.

Tornadoes generally have wind speeds much higher than hurricanes. But hurricanes cause more damage because they are bigger and last much longer.

In addition to tornadoes, flooding can be deadly after a hurricane hits land. Flooding from Hurricane Diane caused 200 deaths and millions of dollars of damage in 1955. The storm brought 10 to 20 inches (25 to 51 centimeters) of rain to parts of Pennsylvania, New York, and New England.

Route 87 in Port Arthur, Texas, was underwater following Hurricane Rita in 2005.

Ranking the Forceful Winds

Scientists rank hurricanes to give people an idea of the intensity of the storm. Hurricanes are ranked using the Saffir-Simpson Hurricane Wind Scale. A Category 1 hurricane has the least forceful winds. A Category 5 hurricane has the most forceful.

Each time a hurricane goes up a notch on the scale, the damage it causes increases by a factor of four. For example, a Category 2 hurricane causes four times as much damage as a Category 1 hurricane.

Category	Wind Speed	Damage	Example
Category 1	74 to 95 mph (119 to 153 kph)	Minor damage to trees and mobile homes	Hurricane Cindy, 2005
Category 2	96 to 110 mph (154 to 177 kph)	Major damage to mobile homes and minor damage to small buildings	Hurricane Frances, 2004
Category 3	111 to 130 mph (179 to 209 kph)	Moderate damage to small buildings; some trees uprooted or snapped	Hurricane Rita, 2005
Category 4	131 to 155 mph (211 to 249 kph)	Major damage to small buildings; many trees uprooted or snapped	Hurricane Charley, 2004
Category 5	> 155 mph (> 249 kph)	Extreme damage to or destruction of buildings and trees	Hurricane Andrew, 1992

Hurricane wind gusts can be up to 25 percent higher than the storm's top average wind speed. These sudden, brief wind bursts last less than 20 seconds.

A hurricane may receive several rankings as the storm's power increases and decreases. The historical ranking a hurricane receives is based on its intensity when it hits land. Hurricane Katrina strengthened to a Category 5 storm over the Gulf of Mexico. But when it hit land in southeastern Louisiana, it had weakened to a Category 3 storm. Therefore, Katrina is ranked as a Category 3 hurricane.

Pine trees in Florida were snapped by the force of Hurricane Andrew's Category 5 winds.

Chapter 2

PREDICTING A HURRICANE

Hurricane Season

Most hurricanes develop during a period known as hurricane season. In the eastern Pacific Ocean, hurricane season lasts from May 15 to November 30. In the western Pacific and south Indian Ocean, most of these powerful storms form between early January and late March. And in the Atlantic region, this period lasts from June 1 until November 30. Ninety-six percent of major hurricanes occur during these months.

January–March

INDIAN OCEAN

January–March

 area where most hurricanes form

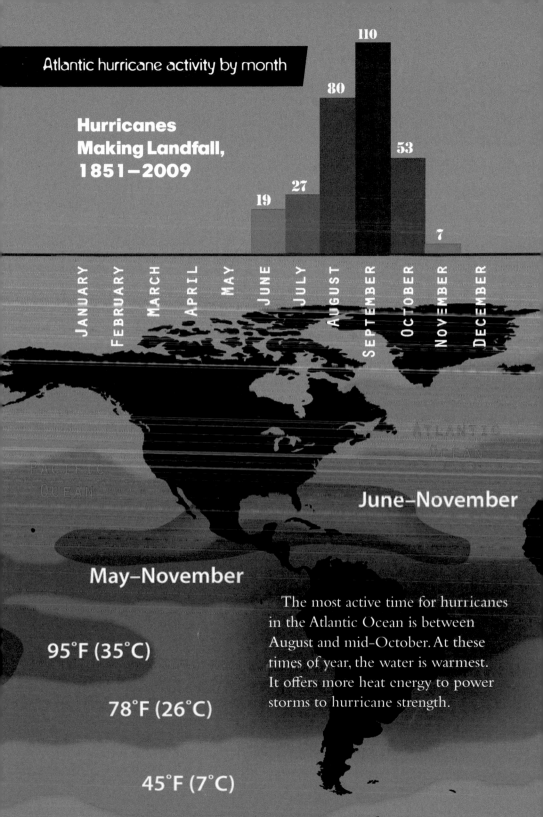

Atlantic hurricane activity by month

Hurricanes Making Landfall, 1851–2009

JANUARY	FEBRUARY	MARCH	APRIL	MAY	JUNE	JULY	AUGUST	SEPTEMBER	OCTOBER	NOVEMBER	DECEMBER
					19	27	80	110	53	7	

June–November

May–November

95°F (35°C)

78°F (26°C)

45°F (7°C)

45°F (-2°C)

The most active time for hurricanes in the Atlantic Ocean is between August and mid-October. At these times of year, the water is warmest. It offers more heat energy to power storms to hurricane strength.

ATLANTIC OCEAN

PACIFIC OCEAN

Tracking Hurricanes

A satellite captured an image of Hurricane Jeanne, the deadliest hurricane of 2004.

Weather forecasters watch for conditions that can cause hurricanes. They let people know when a hurricane is likely to strike and where it will probably come ashore. They also predict how strong it may be.

Weather forecasters keep an eye on tropical disturbances and storms that could strengthen. **Satellites** take pictures from space that provide information about wind speed, cloud formation, and air temperature.

Crews in ships and airplanes measure air pressure and wind speed. Forecasters also get data from weather instruments that send information. They use **radar** to look at storms that get close to shore.

Data about weather conditions helps forecasters predict which path the storm will take. But predicting where the storm will go is not an easy task. Hurricanes don't move in a straight line or follow the paths of past storms. The direction a storm takes is affected by many things. Weather conditions can change quickly, making hurricane prediction difficult.

Tropical Depression
Tropical Storm
Hurricane
Major Hurricane

Hurricane Jeanne took a looping path through the Bahamas before hitting the United States.

ATLANTIC OCEAN

satellite—a spacecraft that circles Earth; satellites take pictures of Earth from space
radar—a system that uses radio waves to detect and locate objects

Hurricane Hunters

Imagine flying into a hurricane's dark clouds. The airplane rises and falls as it is pelted by hail and rain. Everything shakes as the plane is pushed by the wind. The next second, everything is peaceful. Rain stops and the sky is blue. Then the plane flies back into the fierce winds and driving rain.

EYE OF THE
HURRICANE

Hurricane hunters help forecasters predict where a hurricane is going. First they fly into a storm during its early stages. They look to see which direction the winds are blowing. In the Atlantic Ocean, storms with counterclockwise winds could turn into a hurricane. When the storm gains strength, the hurricane hunters fly right through the center.

The first time a pilot flew into a hurricane was 1943. Lieutenant Joseph B. Duckworth flew into a hurricane off Texas.

Lockheed-Martin's WP-3D Orion, known as the P-3, is among the airplanes most frequently used by hurricane hunters.

Crews fly through the storm again and again to collect weather data. They release tube-shaped devices that measure the wind direction and speed. These devices, called dropsondes, also measure air pressure, temperature, and humidity. They send data to the crew in the airplane and to the National Hurricane Center (NHC). Scientists at the NHC study hurricanes and other tropical storms. They use the data to learn how fast the storm is moving and where it is heading.

Hurricane Researchers

Hurricane forecasters are always trying to make their predictions better. People depend on forecasts to help them escape a hurricane's destruction.

At a research center near Miami, Florida, scientists at the NHC gather information about present weather conditions. They also study past data. They want to understand why and how these storms form, grow, and fall apart. Their work has improved the way people measure the intensity of storms. It has also helped people better predict what the storms will do.

Forecasters at the NHC use radar data to track storms.

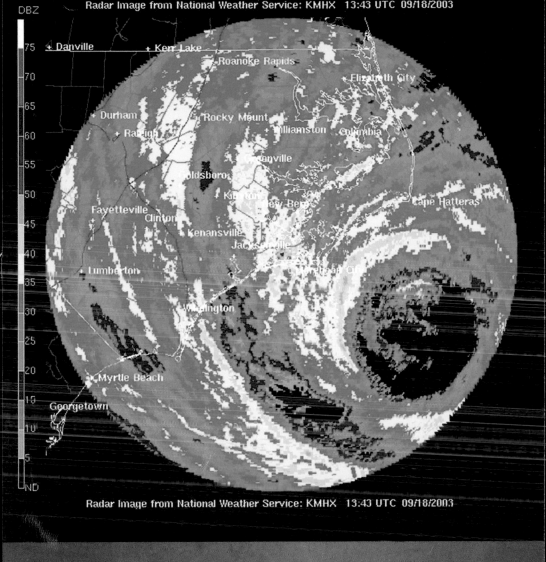

DBZ

75
70
65
60
55
50
45
40
35
30
25
20
15
10
5
ND

+ Danville
+ Kerr Lake
+ Roanoke Rapids
+ Elizabeth City
+ Durham
+ Rocky Mount
+ Williamston
Columbia
+ Raleigh
Greenville
Goldsboro
Cape Hatteras
Fayetteville
Kinston
New Bern
Clinton
Kenansville
Jacksonville
Lumberton
Morehead City
Wilmington
Myrtle Beach
Georgetown

Radar Image from National Weather Service: KMHX 13:43 UTC 09/18/2003

The NHC is part of the National Oceanic and Atmospheric Administration. Researchers who work for this group study the ocean and the atmosphere. Mathematicians, **meteorologists**, and other scientists all work together. Their work helps people understand the many factors that create nature's violent storms.

meteorologist—a scientist who studies Earth's climate and weather

27

Chapter 3

THE WORST HURRICANES

The Deadliest

Many of the deadliest hurricanes to hit the United States came ashore more than 100 years ago. At that time, it was difficult for forecasters to tell when and where a storm would hit. Few tools were available to help forecasters with their predictions. Forecasters also lacked a way to warn most people about the coming danger.

Thousands of people went to the Superdome in New Orleans to take refuge from Hurricane Katrina.

But even when people know a dangerous hurricane is approaching, they may still be helpless. Forecasters predicted Hurricane Katrina would slam into New Orleans on August 25, 2005. However, few thought that levees would break and flood the city. People who could not leave in time had no way to escape the rising water. Many people drowned in the floods that covered many Gulf Coast communities.

Hurricane	Year	Category	Death Toll
1. Galveston, Texas	1000	4	8,000 to 12,000
2. Southeastern Florida, Lake Okeechobee	1928	4	2,500 to 3,000
3. Katrina (Louisiana, Mississippi, Alabama, Florida, and Georgia)	2005	3	1,500
4. Cheniere Caminanda, Louisiana	1893	4	1,100 to 1,140
5. Sea Islands, South Carolina, and Georgia	1893	3	1,000

The Costliest

Hurricanes rip apart buildings and send trees and power line poles crashing down. Roads become covered with floodwaters and blocked by debris. Homes are battered by winds, soaked by rain, and flooded with water. Families can lose everything.

BOATING WOES

Hurricane Andrew severely damaged thousands of boats docked in marinas in southern Florida. The storm lifted them from their anchors. When the water went back down, the vessels were found on docks, highways, and people's lawns. At one marina, a pile of powerboats looked like stacked dominoes. The storm is estimated to have caused $500 million in damage to boats alone.

When Hurricane Andrew hit the Bahamas, southern Florida, and Louisiana in 1992, it left more than 100,000 people homeless. The storm destroyed thousands of homes and businesses. Hurricane Andrew also damaged hundreds of schools.

The Costliest Hurricanes

1. KATRINA
2005
CATEGORY 3
$81 BILLION IN DAMAGE

Hurricane Wilma's Category 3 winds blew out the windows of many Florida buildings.

2. ANDREW
1992
CATEGORY 5
$26.5 BILLION IN DAMAGE

3. WILMA
2005
CATEGORY 3
$20.6 BILLION IN DAMAGE

4. CHARLEY
2004
CATEGORY 4
$15 BILLION IN DAMAGE

5. IVAN
2004
CATEGORY 3
$14.2 BILLION IN DAMAGE

The Most Intense

A hurricane's intensity is measured by its air pressure. Air may seem weightless, but it presses down on Earth. Because the warm air in a hurricane is rising, it puts less pressure on the planet's surface. The stronger the storm, the lower its air pressure will be.

The area of lowest pressure in a hurricane is at the center of the storm. The hurricane spins quickly to try to fill this low pressure area. It draws up moisture, releases heat, and creates more thunderstorms as it turns.

```
5. INDIANOLA, TEXAS
   1886
   CATEGORY 4
   MINIMUM AIR PRESSURE:
   27.31 INCHES (69.37 CM)
```

An instrument called a barometer is used to measure air pressure. Air pressure forces mercury in the barometer into a tube, where it is measured in inches. Normal air pressure at sea level is about 30 inches (76.2 cm) of mercury.

Two of the three most intense hurricanes hit land within 50 miles (80 km) of each other. Hurricane Katrina hit land at Buras, Louisiana, in 2005. Hurricane Camille slammed into Bay St. Louis, Mississippi, in 1969.

2. CAMILLE
1969
CATEGORY 5
MINIMUM AIR PRESSURE:
26.84 INCHES (68.17 CM)

4. ANDREW
1992
CATEGORY 5
MINIMUM AIR PRESSURE:
27.23 INCHES (69.16 CM)

3. KATRINA
2005
CATEGORY 3
MINIMUM AIR PRESSURE:
27.17 INCHES (69.01 CM)

1. FLORIDA KEYS ("LABOR DAY")
1935
CATEGORY 5
MINIMUM AIR PRESSURE:
26.35 INCHES (66.93 CM)

CHAPTER 4

THE AFTERMATH

Coping After the Storm

After a hurricane, it's not back to life as usual for people affected by the storm. Houses may be without roofs. Walls may have collapsed. Entire buildings may be reduced to rubble. Even people whose homes survived may be without power for days. Sometimes food is unsafe to eat and water is unsafe to drink.

FACT: More than 1.7 million people along the Gulf of Mexico lost power after Hurricane Katrina. Some were without electricity for weeks.

BEFORE

Folly Beach, South Carolina, before Hurricane Hugo, 1989

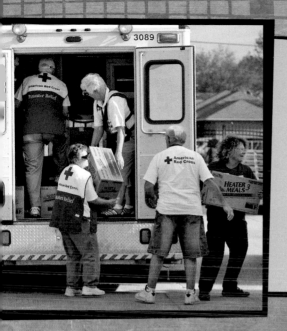

READY TO HELP

When a hurricane strikes, the Red Cross is ready. This group helps people in emergencies. It sets up shelters to house people who have to leave their homes. Red Cross workers provide storm victims with clothing, food, and medicine. They help families contact friends and loved ones to let them know they are safe.

Floods may make roads impossible to drive on. Many roads will be blocked by trees, building materials, and other debris. Damaged bridges could collapse under the weight of a car.

Folly Beach, South Carolina, after Hurricane Hugo, 1989

Rebuilding

In areas hit by a hurricane, people don't give up. They rebuild the homes, businesses, and roads destroyed by the storm. They don't build them exactly as they were before, however. They use new ideas and make them even stronger.

After Hurricane Katrina hit, homes in New Orleans were built higher off the ground. Some apartment buildings are now built with parking garages on the bottom floor. If another hurricane hits, the parking garages will flood instead of people's homes.

VOLUNTEERS REBUILD

Volunteers from all over the country have helped rebuild homes along the Gulf Coast that were destroyed by hurricanes Katrina and Rita in 2005. Habitat for Humanity builds homes for low-income families. Habitat volunteers began building in October 2005, six weeks after Katrina hit. That was the start of an ongoing effort. Since then, thousands of volunteers have helped pound nails and raise walls. More than 1,300 homes have been built in the region through Habitat for Humanity.

The Highway 90 bridge between Biloxi and Ocean Springs, Mississippi, was ripped apart by Hurricane Katrina. A new bridge connecting the cities was built taller than the old one. Its roadbed is higher than even the tallest waves of a hurricane. The blocks on the bottom of the bridge have been designed so they will not be pushed off their supports by forceful waves.

The Highway 90 bridge between Biloxi and Ocean Springs, Mississippi

Environmental Impact

The landscape takes a beating during a hurricane. Winds rip off tree limbs and entire trees topple. Islands disappear under floodwaters. Waves tear at the shoreline, gouging out chunks of land.

NATURAL HURRICANE BUFFER

Wetlands along the coast provide natural protection against hurricane damage. They absorb the rising water brought in by a storm surge. This protects the surrounding land from flooding.

But wetlands are in danger. They have been harmed by people and natural disasters. Levees channel river water away from wetlands. Severe storms rip away plants.

However, rebuilding projects are bringing wetlands back. Levees are being improved. Plants are being replaced. The wetlands are slowly coming back to offer protection from the floodwaters that a hurricane brings.

Trees in Slidell, Louisiana, were ripped out by the roots during Hurricane Katrina in 2005.

Animals try to escape the storm. Dolphins swim into open water. Snakes, bears, and foxes head for higher ground. But rising water and whipping winds doom some animals. Rabbits and muskrats drown when their dens are flooded.

Fish suffer too. Surging waves churn the ocean floor, ripping up their **habitat**. And oil spills pollute the water when storage tanks are damaged by the storm. Eventually, though, the environment begins to recover.

habitat—a place and conditions in which an animal lives

Chapter 5

PREPARING FOR A HURRICANE

Watches and Warnings

The National Weather Service issues watches and warnings to alert people about possible hurricanes. A watch means the area could be hit by a hurricane within the next 36 hours. A warning means a hurricane is expected to arrive in 24 hours or less.

Local radio and TV stations broadcast storm updates to keep people informed. If a hurricane watch is issued, people should begin to prepare for a hurricane. They should stock up on supplies they might need during the storm. People also need to protect their homes and belongings from the storm. Their cars should be full of gas in case they need to evacuate.

FACT

There are an average of eight to nine tropical storms and hurricanes in the Atlantic Ocean each year.

Making sure you have an adequate supply of clean drinking water is an important step in preparing for a hurricane.

During a hurricane warning, people should listen to the radio or TV for updated hurricane reports. Officials will continue to broadcast advice to help them decide on the safest place to be during a storm. Sometimes people's homes are in danger of being damaged by floods or strong winds. They then need to evacuate to escape the storm.

evacuate—to move away from an area because of danger there

Stocking Up for a Storm

Families who live in areas where a hurricane may strike need to be ready. At the beginning of each hurricane season, family members should gather items they will need during and after a storm. A hurricane may cut off power, make water undrinkable, or make it impossible to get out for food or supplies. Here are some supplies to have ready:

- evacuation map with two possible routes to your destination

- instructions on how to turn off your home's electricity, water, and gas

- a first-aid kit and important medications

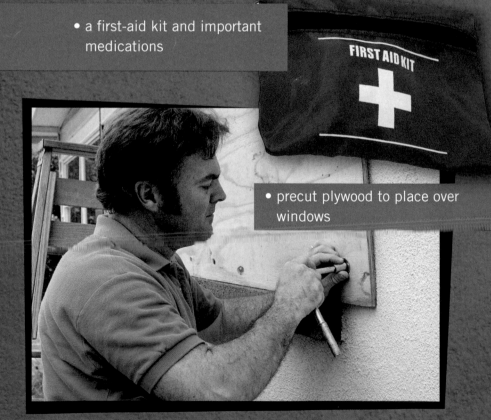

- precut plywood to place over windows

• water—1 gallon (3.8 liters) per person per day

• canned food and a can opener

• fire extinguisher

• flashlight

• protective clothing, rainwear, and bedding or sleeping bags

• toilet paper

• insect repellent

• duct tape, tarp, and rope

• the name, address, and phone number of an out-of-area contact person

• a battery-powered radio and extra batteries

Planning for Disaster

A family should also prepare by creating a disaster plan. Family members need to decide how they will reach each other if a hurricane strikes. They should plan what to do in case they have to evacuate. The local emergency planning office can tell people if they live in an area that could flood during a hurricane. A family may plan to stay with friends, go to a motel, or use a Red Cross shelter.

As Hurricane Gustav approached the Gulf Coast in August 2008, the southbound lane of I-10 West was closed to allow more traffic to travel north.

CARING FOR YOUR PET

When making a hurricane disaster plan for yourself, make one for your pet as well. If you will be at home during the storm, make sure you have a supply of food and water for your pet.

If you need to go to a shelter, find out which ones allow animals. Some shelters are pet-friendly. Other shelters arrange for pets to be kept at a separate place nearby.

Shelters require that pets have a collar and rabies tag, so make sure your pet has been **vaccinated**. Pets need to be brought to the shelter in a carrier or cage, so be sure to have one on hand.

Hurricane forecasts have improved, and buildings have been made stronger. But people still need to be alert to hurricane watches and warnings. Hurricanes can sweep away everything in their path. Being aware of a hurricane's approach gives you time to escape the fury of this dangerous storm.

to protect against a disease by injecting dead or weakened germs into a person or animal

GLOSSARY

atmosphere (AT-muhss-fihr)—the mass of air surrounding Earth

condense (kuhn-DENSS)—to turn from a gas into a liquid

cyclone (SYE-clone)—a storm system spinning around a defined center of low pressure

debris (duh-BREE)—the remains of something that has been destroyed

evacuate (i-VAK-yoo-ate)—to move away from an area because of danger there

habitat (HAB-uh-tat)—the place and conditions in which an animal lives

high tide (HYE TIDE)—high sea level caused by the pull of the sun and the moon on Earth

levee (LEV-ee)—a bank built up to prevent flooding

meteorologist (mee-tee-ur-OL-oh-jist)—a scientist who studies Earth's climate and weather

radar (RAY-dar)—a system that uses radio waves to detect and locate objects

satellite (SAT-uh-lite)—a spacecraft that circles Earth; satellites take pictures of Earth from space

storm surge (STORM SURJ)—a dome of water pushed by a hurricane

tropics (TROP-iks)—the extremely hot area of Earth near the equator

vaccinate (VAK-suh-nate)—to protect against a disease by injecting dead or weakened germs into a person or animal

READ MORE

Demarest, Chris L. *Hurricane Hunters: Riders on the Storm*. New York: Margaret K. McElderry Books, 2006.

Nardo, Don. *Storm Surge: The Science of Hurricanes*. Headline Science. Mankato, Minn.: Compass Point Books, 2009.

Pietras, Jamie. *Hurricane Katrina*. Great Historic Disasters. New York: Chelsea House, 2008.

Royston, Angela. *Hurricanes and Tornadoes*. Wild Weather. Mankato, Minn.: QEB Publishing, 2008.

INTERNET SITES

FactHound offers a safe, fun way to find Internet sites related to this book. All of the sites on FactHound have been researched by our staff.

Here's all you do:

Visit *www.facthound.com*

Type in this code: 9781429647953

INDEX